"What fidelity to place, memory, history, and heart. His poems burn us, feed us, and make us feel beloved even if we have been broken. Language, as he uses it, holds us and leads us to a place where we can mourn and pray and wonder. Wow, I say again and again, as I turn the pages and then turn back again to savour what has been so carefully and painfully written."
—LORNA CROZIER, author of *What the Soul Doesn't Want*

"Randy Lundy's poems carry the immediacy and radiance and intelligence of the lived world itself. His embodied, enstoried singing casts a precise and multiplying light into his own life, and into the lives of all beings with whom we share this earth."—JANE HIRSHFIELD, author of *The Beauty*

"More than poems, these are offerings and songs, deep magma in winter, earth and all directions of our lives and the surrounding world. They are grounded constellations created of fire and ice, hunger and fullness, extreme differences brought together. More than words, these works are our breath and a miraculously remembered future. Lundy's words create a domain of signals that reveal ways the human and earth are one body."—LINDA HOGAN, author of *Dark. Sweet.: New and Selected Poems*

"Randy Lundy has entered the place where the masters reside. His poems join the shades that walk among them. There aren't many people who get to that place and sometimes it can feel very lonely there, but the masters are saved by the brilliant and humble work they have done, their poems the crevices in our lives where the light shines through."—PATRICK LANE, author of *Washita*

"Randy Lundy's poems bring forward the spirit of his Cree ancestry, and place our species humbly among the creatures of Earth—who are all observed with deep reverence and perceptive care. We should be grateful to him for bringing his wise, wry, visionary, large-hearted meditations into language, and for demonstrating the need for 'seeing with another kind of eye.' A book to read and be read by."—DON MᶜKAY, author of *Strike/Slip*

"'Memory is an uncomfortable skin.' A private thought. Too private to keep?... What does Lundy want of memory? A grain of sand. Its magnitude too vast to conceive. So much, too much. Bird eggs. Stones. Clouds. Fur glisten. To keep, to be kept by. Never mind colonization. Even though it matters. Even though we must mind.... Read, yes, we must, Randy Lundy's *Blackbird Song*. It calls to us."—SIMON J. ORTIZ, author of *from Sand Creek* and *The People Shall Continue*

BLACKBIRD SONG

ᐅᓂᐸ

OSKANA POETRY & POETICS

Randy Lundy

Blackbird Song

University of Regina Press

© 2018 Randy Lundy

All rights reserved. No part of this work covered by the copyrights hereon may be reproduced or used in any form or by any means—graphic, electronic, or mechanical—without the prior written permission of the publisher. Any request for photocopying, recording, taping or placement in information storage and retrieval systems of any sort shall be directed in writing to Access Copyright.

Printed and bound in Canada at Marquis. The text of this book is printed on 100% post-consumer recycled paper with earth-friendly vegetable-based inks.

Cover and text design: Duncan Campbell, University of Regina Press

Proofreader: Kristine Douaud

Cover art: "Line art drawing of a Red-winged Blackbird" by Pearson Scott Foresman / Wikimedia Commons / Public Domain

The text and titling faces are Arno, designed by Robert Slimbach.

Library and Archives Canada Cataloguing in Publication

Lundy, Randy, 1967-, author
    Blackbird song / Randy Lundy.

(Oskana poetry & poetics)
Poems.
Issued in print and electronic formats.

ISBN 978-0-88977-557-2 (softcover).—ISBN 978-0-88977-558-9 (PDF)

I. Title. II. Series: Oskana poetry & poetics

PS8573.U54398B53 2018   C811'.54
C2018-901576-4   C2018-901577-2

10 9 8 7 6 5 4 3 2 1

UNIVERSITY OF REGINA PRESS
University of Regina
Regina, Saskatchewan
Canada S4S 0A2
TELEPHONE: (306) 585-4758
FAX: (306) 585-4699
WEB: www.uofrpress.ca
EMAIL: uofrpress@uregina.ca

We acknowledge the support of the Canada Council for the Arts for our publishing program. We acknowledge the financial support of the Government of Canada. / Nous reconnaissons l'appui financier du gouvernement du Canada. This publication was made possible with support from Creative Saskatchewan's Creative Industries Production Grant Program.

for Reta & Jim Lundy

CONTENTS

Mankind owns four things
That are no good at sea.
Anchor, rudder, oars,
And the fear of going down.

ANTONIO MACHADO

I

Constellation after Constellation,

Turning on the Spears of Trees

JANUARY

The dead of winter.
I am thinking
of my mother.

She exists for me
the way the owl

perches
on black spruce
backlit by streetlight
grey against night sky

just before taking flight.

FOR YOUR LOVER ON THE EVE OF HER THIRTY-FIFTH BIRTHDAY

Across the rise and fall of prairie, through sage, wolf willow,
and wild rose, a coyote follows its nose toward a meal of field mice.
Occasionally it raises its voice in answer to a distant train.

Two miles east of where you sit with coffee and cigarette,
in the coulees leading down to Cottonwood Creek,
a pair of Great Pyrenees guard sheep.

Night comes swiftly like the wing of a blackbird.

Your eyelids are drooping petals, soon you will sleep,
dreaming of an old woman beneath freshly turned earth,
her body not yet settled, like a stone finding its ease.

You will dream yourself into a new kind of creature, a few lines
at the corners of the eyes or mouth, which were not there before.
When you rise you will not recognize the animal you have become.

When you wake, in order to go on, you will have to reaffirm
We cannot live our lives like the saints, dwelling at the centre
of a flame or sitting by a spring listening to its eschatological voice.

Assigning names to the few things we still recognize, tiny feathered
bodies catch our eyes like hooks, their beaks and claws
the closest thing to angels that will visit us on this day.

American redstart, Swainson's thrush, brown thrasher.
Still, in the mythological night, transfiguration has come.
Fire and bread and, if we are lucky, a small measure of love.

Leaves on the mountain ash have fallen—
bare branches
like your shoulders when I met you

in the spring.

A PRAYER

Morning then and there in that other season—
redpolls, golden finches, splotches and streaks of colour among
heavy-scented blossoms, red-winged blackbird song from the bulrushes.
Beyond the edge of the dugout at the north end of town
a single meadowlark fluting in the fast-ripening field.

At the edge of and from beyond
a geography with which you are acquainted.

Midwinter this afternoon, Cape Breton clay cup
of tea, cracked glaze of that island
once joined to Africa.

This morning you filled the feeder with seeds after finding
the year's first frozen bird—a song sparrow, female,
stiff with hunger.

You learned from your grandmother to make such offerings.
Afterward, you lit a candle in front of the black and white
photo of that woman
holding a small, brown boy on her knees—

Kindle this fire, beeswax candle, offer a simple prayer.
Do these things in memory of me.

You remember the kitchen drawer
where she kept a wire coil notebook
recording in neat columns
the temperatures, daytime high and low,
and sky conditions—

as if knowing could change what had been
or predict what was to come.

WOMAN WHO TAUGHT HER GRANDSON TO LOVE

One day the entries stopped
sudden as the heart
in a palm-sized
feathered body

at forty below zero.

FOR KOHKUM, RETA

Might as well settle
in a hard-heavy chair,
with a mug of steaming
green tea and some Powwow or
plainchant turned up loud.
Stare out the window
into the glare of sun glazing
the snowfield south of the house.

Remember the butter-glazed, golden
crust of bread fresh from the oven.
Remember the oven door
creaking, heat blasting
your six-year-old face.

Your body's a canvas and bone lodge,
stone-glow hot in your belly.

Low sun at noon falls lower.
Sparrows huddle at the feeder at dusk.

Tonight, a mile north of here,
a train engine will groan and then roar,
a biblical beast, a wihtikow come for the feast.

Memory is an uncomfortable skin.

Your mind like a sapling, bent,
curved like the earth.
Curved like a question mark.

Remember that woman.
It's always a woman
with white hands or brown hands.
The kitchen, mid-winter frost on the windows
as you wait for the school bus,
that smell: yeast and wheat.
Love, was it?
Birth?

O Grandmother, O Mother, O Lover,
O Woman who birthed
the elliptic egg of the universe.

Beneath your feet,
aquifer-pulse.
Somewhere deeper,
magma-flow.

The geologically slow
shift and drift
of the continent.

Nothing else you can do, really, friend.
The elm tree is busy with its own season's work
and has no time for your stories. It's paying you
no mind. It's autumn, the tree is closing up
shop for the winter. *Autumn* is far too high-minded
a word. The tree prefers *fall*, leaves tumbling, one by one.
The tree deep in concentration. You might think
it's a simple matter to let go, but the tree
knows what it takes to shed everything.
You have worked hard to acquire offerings
even if nothing more than a few slender,
green, heart-shaped leaves.

The fall after you lost your father, you grieved.
Everything you have done since has been grieving:
making a cup of tea, a meal, or holding that woman's wrist.
Concentrating on the blood branches that lead deeper
into her body, that lead, finally, to roots. That's how
you want to know her. What is it you want today?

A bit of pity perhaps. Be thankful for what you have.
If you stop your own moaning for just a moment,
you can hear each leaf pressing itself down
like a hand to warm the cooling earth.

It is the first day of November.
All the leaves are down.
Still the north-west wind persists.

FASTING

Set yourself this one task:
to grow thin like the moon.

Sit on this glacial-sand hilltop,
listen to the coyotes raise
their voices.

Each time the stars reveal themselves,
the night sun recedes further
into the darkening penumbra
of her veil.

Still,
somewhere in darkness
she continues to burn.

There are times when you think
it's no use. You know
it's a trick you do
only with words.

Nothing grows thinner than your own
thin disguise.
You have sat here four nights.
Now, you begin to feel
you have been here before.

Perhaps there is hope
you might learn still
how to be alone, how your tongue
can curl like a flame to take
the shape of what it desires
and burns.

Perhaps you can learn
how to refrain from the urge
to take back home that self
you think you know.

for Leonard

The mountain breathes clouds,
dragon-smoke, like the breath
of an inferno. The mountains
thinking themselves into being.
Thinking magma-flow, thinking
the liquid fire at the core of
everything.
        Thinking mountains
and valleys and rivers. Singing.

Warm, humid air, cooling fast
as it climbed the western slope,
now plunging down the east
like a landslide toward the lake,
like an escaped ski skimming
between finely needled pines,
over snow-tipped waves, bare-faced
rock outcroppings.

           Your own mind,
too, a kind of outcropping, a shifting
of deep plates, and the thrust
of the sharp-bladed range into
the sky of everything you are not.

THE CHAIR BY THE DOOR

A chair is an invitation.
Think of how many times
you have passed it by
sitting there near the door
without considering its nature.

Every morning,
every evening,
it's here watching
you depart or arrive
quietly biding its time
like a well-trained dog.

Despite its four strong legs,
it is not a dog. Do not think
abiding patience means
it has been trained or tamed.
Tell it to sit or fetch,
you'll be greeted
with an unchanging
straight ahead moon-
blank stare.

It is still
an oak, dreaming branches
that spread into blue,
remembering leaves.
It contemplates how
its body is transfigured
rain and light.

Move it around
from room to room,
up and down the stairs.
It always feels the grip of roots.

Perhaps this is what draws
a man toward its seat
while waiting for
the birth or the death
of someone he will always love.

Late June, the crabapples
in full bloom—

Light west wind, and each petal falls
this quietly—

The gleaming blackbirds stop
their eager chattering—

Watch each petal
drop.

THE CACTUS

You sit in the forgotten bone-dry hills
surrounded by sand and sagebrush
above Buffalo Pound Lake.

A day and a night, and then
three more days and nights.
Do not mark the hours. Just sit
until the prickly pear raises its bloom.

A pale thing, translucent moon, sea anemone,
the first thin veil of a cataract that will lead a man
to the necessity of seeing with another kind of eye.

Can you birth a thing like this flower?
Elemental, composed of water and light.
The concentrated effort of pure will.

The blossom wilts and drops
without sadness, nothing resembling
nostalgia or regret.

AUTUMN ELMS

Dawn was a slow undressing
of the trees, revealing slender arms and
elbows, above thicker legs and knees.

I don't think they were embarrassed
lined up along the street fronting my house.

They waved their limbs in the morning
breeze, chilly though it was, greeted
the sunrise with their nakedness and sang.

The sun cheered them on, and
perhaps it should have been me
embarrassed for being a voyeur
standing at the kitchen window,
breath frosting the glass.

Fully clothed, stationary,
not singing.

HAPPINESS

after Jane Kenyon

It's true what the dying woman said,
there's no accounting for happiness.

No matter the good will you have spent
trying the patience of family and friends,
some of whom have died. Never mind
that every time you dig deep in your pockets
you find those cold, bright coins
of anger and regret.

Sparrows gather daily at the feeder
you have hung in the elm tree in the backyard
and at the earthen bowl you will fill with water
for their raucous bathing.

Sleek, bright wings glisten in the sun.
They have no shame.

SOLACE

for Shirley Johnson

We buried her, and as morning turned into afternoon,
I remember staring out the picture window of her family's
living room, across the highway to the expanse of prairie
with its coulees rising into hills, and waves
of heat shimmering above parched dirt.

Or was the movement that I sensed
a small herd of pronghorn, seven slender bodies moving
gracefully over the lip of the world, to feed and drink
somewhere beyond my seeing.

I cannot be sure, though I know you might need
something more certain. Please understand that certainty
won't ease your grief. If she were to arrive today
on my back step, she'd smile to see me.

Sitting here, drinking tea, looking out the kitchen window
into the backyard, I see a deepening green in the leaves
of the mountain ash and catch the scent
of lilacs blooming in the shade.

While the pale, red poppy petals
seem as if they will tear away in the breeze,
the stalks of the sunflowers are thick enough
to hold their swaying heads, the flare
and weight of those ten thousand seeds.

Here the trees hold the stars
in their spheres. This neither a metaphor,
nor a clever trick. It is simply what to fear
from wind when the cliffs step forward,
fall into emptiness.

There is no need for you
to quiet your mind, to shrink your soul
like a drought-dormant root to fit
the coulee's begging bowl.
The coyote and buffalo rubbing-stone
pay no heed. The restless dead
wander through pine shadows muttering,
unable to hear your desperate invocations.

Even if they could, they would not pause
but simply vanish into the moon-soaked night
like the white-tailed deer on gleaming hooves
stepping into the mist and darkness, leaving
opposing crescent glyphs in wet earth.

Constellation after constellation turning
on the spears of the trees.

BENEDICTION

Late December sunshine,
a forty-kilometer-an-hour wind
warm out of the west scatters crabapples
in the backyard across a thick crust of snow.
Thin-skinned fruit breaks and bleeds
in the glinting beaks of the dozen waxwings
shouting their ecstasy at the bare branches
which snag the blue day's few thin clouds.

Later, lying in bed just before sleep,
your lover's body alongside you
like a warm front in spring
moving westward across the prairie,
in the darkness of your inner ear
those voices—*tsee, tsee, tsee.*

You dream of twelve cinnamon-crested
birds with black throats, of tiny seeds
planted and sprouting songs
deep in grey-brown bellies.

GRACE

All afternoon alone on the lake,
August, and the heat of the sun
setting ablaze the water's surface,
glacial star exploding in your eyes.

The last fish of the day,
a sixteen-inch northern pike
alongside the canoe, exhausted
from the tug and pull of the line,

quiet now after the fight,
fins feathering the water
as it rolls on its side, blind
to the creature who has hauled it
into air, stunned by the breadth of sky,
a passing gull, the afternoon moon.

Later, on the Precambrian beach
of a small pine-spined island,
the chill of evening on your skin,
a small fire and the fish frying.
On your tongue,
taste of stone and cold water.

MIRACLES

What did you see?

In the distance, twenty or twenty-five miles to the southwest,
the hills rising toward the horizon, a pod of humpbacks
travelling the prairie, carrying bits of flint chipped
from arrowheads in their bellies, their sides scarred
with teepee rings.

What did you hear?

In my backyard, three flickers—
male, female, and offspring—probing
the October-brittle grass with elegant beaks,
mostly silent except for an occasional
soft drumming. The breeze rustling
the twin rows of sunflowers.

Is there anything else you can tell us?

In my small flower bed, there was a single poppy,
its four pale petals the rust rose of the sun setting in the hills.
The chambers of a heart in the seasonal retreat of light.
I saw that, too. I saw its round black eye
blink. I heard it breathe.

THE LONG WALK

for Jan

You pause
to sit on the path.
Your companion,
or other walkers
who happen by,
might ask why
you are sitting.

You feel the June-warm,
just-before-it-turns-
cool, evening air
settle down
around you,
lying near enough
that you feel
its breathing
like a dog
with its head
resting in your lap.

Marsh wrens and warblers
flit in the willows;
a single kingbird
perched; in the distance,
three pintails angling up
over a stand of thin aspen,
their departure
still written on
the pond's surface;
and high in the pale
blue, the slash and cut
of feeding swallows.

A three-quarter
waxing moon
like a blank eye
meditating on the last,
now-fading light.

You might reply, *This is a long walk, one that pauses, then keeps on walking,* or *The walk has its own mind, and, right now, it wants to sit,* or *The walk is a journey of the spirit carried by the body like a good friend, and sitting is an important part of the walking.*

You might say any of these things.
Or, you might just sit.

GNOSIS

Elm tree in autumn
letting go of everything, a surrender
of leaves, like keys falling
from a hand, will and necessity become
indistinguishable.

There is no magic word.
The door is locked for the season
and will not open.

It is the same tree in winter,
not asleep, but meditating.
Deep thinking at the core.
You can knock but no one will come.
Motionlessness, nothing but stone
at the base of its rooted tongue.

This tree in spring,
budding and unfurling
its many green eyes,
that door opening.

You might think the elm tree
in summer is awake, but now
is the time that it dreams—
it is warm water coral, it is
a lung which breathes, it is
a tributary, a creek, it is a river.

One morning
you stumble out the back door
into the yard. A red-tailed hawk
perched on the topmost branch.

It stares at something you cannot see,
then spreads its wings and lifts
away, riding an updraft
into the blazing eastern sun.

CONJUNCTIONS

Birchbark-silver peel of a waning
almost-gone-now moon.
Who is mourning? For what or whom?
Who can remember? Speak or name?

Like the low-winter-snowcloud great grey owl
just above the elm's branch tips, who glides
through your field of vision, disappears
against poplar. Barren, but for hoarfrost.

Everything so hard, late November,
Jupiter and Mars in conjunction. A single
coyote bark shatters the brittle air.
The moon withdraws her ashen face.

Pack a single bag, suitcase
from the thrift shop of the heart.

What to take?
Wren feathers, mouse bones,
a lake-stone speckled like an egg.
Slate-grey late-autumn sky,
maple leaves, fallen and red,
pressed between pages of rain.

Pack sorrow and regret, an ill-fitting
pair of old shoes, and Grace,
the black and tan brindled pup,
muscled, crow-sleek, shiny
as a new penny. Red
ball in her mouth.

This will have to do.

Last October, two birds in the bare-branched green elm
with black caps, grey-blue backs and frost-white faces.

Downy woodpeckers, I said, with all the confidence of middle age.
I don't know how to tell you this, but I was wrong.

The birds with chestnut under tail and nasal plaintive voices.
Yesterday I filled the feeders. The nuthatches are back.

I don't know how I could have made such a mistake.
Although this comes late, I have to ask.

SURRENDER

At each solstice, each equinox,
you renounced all that was not yours:
the sun at noon, the moonrise, each of
the stars composing their own patterns,
each following its own course through the night.
Your blood continued on its way,
churning from heart through veins
back to heart, rushing somewhere
you could never name, on business
you never understood. The seasons
turned, became years beyond what
you were able to count and soon
you grew fine hairs on your ears,
coarse ones from your nose
those on your chin silver
like starlight. Still your eyes blazed,
and you argued against the days,
their noisy passing, how they gathered
the blackbirds into flocks and hurled them
southward, into lands beyond the horizon.

It is autumn again. You do not know
how you came to be here. You lay
your body on the brittle grass, beneath
the bowing apple-heavy branches
bewildered, at last, by the world.
You think you may have been mistaken
every moment of your life until now.
Still and silent, ready to give up claim
even to the dull ache
that has been your soul.

II

*The Path Becomes Narrow,
Slight as a Note
from a Carved Wood Flute*

the coyotes in the stubble-dark, early-October fields gather around
the hand-drum-full-moon and sing, their songs rise like the voices of
ancestors you cannot even name, ancestors who dwell in your bones—
rib and thigh and jaw—at the deep centre, in the dark, dark marrow.

Half-burned, half-blackened, Red Bird wooden matches, burned black
as a Newfoundlander's coat; black as a starless, moonless night; black
as a crow's eye; black as the jack pine left standing after the fire blew
through one northern summer when you were eleven. That and the
mounded ash in the small, round bronze bowl on the marble-topped
altar at the centre of your home. From there the smoke rises and carries
each syllable of all you cannot speak.

There are women who know who and what you are—your
grandmothers, who skinned trapped animals, tanned hides, and cut the
throats of sheep to let them bleed out; your mother who carried you
in her womb, her belly risen like a loaf of bread set in the sun on the
kitchen counter, covered with a red-striped, white tea-towel; your lover
too, though now she is gone, somewhere beyond the horizon, near the
equator, where the sun is hot, the clothes are bright, and cumbia plays in
the town's cobble-stone square.

Whatever it is you think you know about the world, your knowing is
not architectonic like the knowing of the green elm in spring, after its
long, dream-free sleep. Now, its roots and trunk, its branches and leaves
define the space between earth and sky—the beetles in the dirt and the
swallows gliding and cutting, feeding two-hundred feet up in the July-
blue afternoon.

What you know is your own memory scarred into your flesh—your
Irish grandmother holding your father as a child in her lap while he
slept; your mother as a young woman bent from the waist watching
bees adrift in the goldenrod along the slow, brown river, not yet having
dreamed you into being; your lover wrapping your trembling body with

her arms while you sweated out the whisky-fever sickness before you quit, too late to keep her with you.

In the empty space on the wall, from which you have removed her picture, hangs a framed poem that reads, *Now you can go into the dark that lives inside you.*

You remember things you cannot possibly remember, but what you must learn about memory is, no matter what you wish, it illuminates nothing. Now light your offerings. Smudge your heavy, thought-sodden body. Offer tobacco to the flame. Now pray.

Sitting on your back deck, beneath the first-breathing leaves of the
Manitoba maple, smoking and drinking coffee, the male Pyrenees asleep
near your feet. The late-April, half moon, waning. But not waxing, as
if you had a choice, as if the world depended on how you looked at it,
how you might tilt your head, your mind. Tonight, there is only that
slow going-into-darkness. The Big Dipper directly overhead, spilling
almost enough night to swallow the stars. The Big Dipper—*asterism*, not
constellation, you have learned.

Ursa Major. Great Mother Bear, three cubs trailing behind.

Whatever it was you were thinking lost now in the coyotes' yowls from
the fields beyond the edge of town, even that singing drowned out by
the whistle and groan of the diesel engines pulling the train by a block-
and-a-half south.

What was it you were thinking? You were thinking about remembering.
Remembering a small brown-skinned boy in the summer sun in a large
opening among the pine trees, his grandmother's eyes glowing with
pride for no reason other than that he was alive, holding in his small
hands a jute bag of seed potatoes for her garden. The order there. The
straight lines. The love.

Where is your grandfather in this memory? Your father? By this time
your mother was lost to you for the next twenty years.

Maybe what matters is that night and distance have swallowed the train.
You are here, now, with a sleeping dog. The maple trees. The moon's
retreat. The frogs in the flooded ditches along the tracks sing their
gelatinous breeding.

Christmas Eve morning, temperature approaching zero, and an indistinct movement of air, just a trickle, not wind, barely a breath, warm, out of the south. In the front garden a few rounded rocks poke above the snow, the bald heads of monks

—the season, a monastery of silence.

Are you waiting for that feeling—the feeling that the ungraspable, the ineffable is somewhere close by? Friend, stranger, stranger to yourself, are you waiting for the appearance of that something whose appearance would be its own vanishing? A meteorite that flames and drowns.

Remember the season before this season. A windless October afternoon. Nothing but gravity, the weight of the passage of time, to pull down the leaves, like a lone man, now old, pulling down an ancient wooden barn. The sound of a few leaves falling, or just one leaf, or less.

Now, remember farther back. Was there someone you loved, someone who loved you, to whom you did not reveal wherever it was you had been? Was it your father? Your mother? Was it a woman? What is it you may have done, that you may have seen or said, that you now cannot speak?

With what voice you have left, speak in the weightless cadences of someone who has traversed a great distance, whose crossing was hard. Even if not to clear a space for your *self*. Even if every memory, all time before this very moment, the history of yourself, leaves you cold.

Is what cannot be seen, cannot be explained, always elsewhere, invisible, not beneath, but beyond even the signs that point its way? Where did endlessness begin, where has it been? How close has it come to you, sitting here and now in a small stuccoed house on the Canadian prairie?

Turning toward the window, you see it has begun to snow. Everything slowly growing, not white, but grey, and indistinct.

Mid-winter, a grey liturgy of branches against the blue sky, gilded with sunlight.

Like Orpheus on that walk toward the thin light in the distance, you would like to touch the small shoulder-bone of the woman you love— in your desire you forget yourself. This forgetting is a blessing of the flesh.

The woman is gone, but the desire is not, and you are troubled by the thought that memory may be more interesting than the disturbing presence. Perhaps this is the architecture of how and why memory endures. You had hoped the sky would not take you apart. The two of you. You had hoped the sky would not dismantle *You.* You had hoped that what hides itself would be there, still, for you to know.

After dark-fall, the snow begins, but you doubt the snow understands the fruit trees as it buries them. Is this ignorance, or just another species of forgetting? A sound arrives as if from a great distance, *Come, come here*— it is the moon calling to your liquid, moon-washed body, in a voice that sounds like a spirit churning, being poured from pitcher to pitcher, back and forth.

Being empty, what is there but to receive?

In the dark, prairie night, you hear the approach of a freight-train, sounding nothing like patience, perhaps penitence, and if you could see it, you would see an apparent order, car after car arriving and arriving, as if there were no end to the ordered world. Then the sound passes by, recedes into the distance, buries itself deep in the principal night, tender and senseless, and buries itself in its leaving.

In the silence that follows, you can almost hear each flake of snow settling upon the earth, can almost imagine that you sense a mercy that is not your own. Nothing you are, nothing you have been, is irrevocable. Out of your own thoughts come the materials for the beginning of everything; out of your own memory, eventually, comes everything that cannot endure.

When dawn comes, there will be nothing private, personal, or loving about the light—it reveals what it reveals, and too soon after light-fall comes night-rise, and, even in the dawn, there is a darkness gathering in the still-sleeping eyes of our children.

When they wake, the winter-wind will ask of each, *Where is your family, child?*, and bewildered they will not speak, but the wind will answer, across the dormant, frozen fields, its voice a long-stretched sound, like a train-horn in the long-stretched distance.

You are here, understanding or not understanding, not quite sure if it is dawn or dusk in this spider-spun, heft and weft of light.

THE PATH BECOMES NARROW, SLIGHT
AS A NOTE FROM A CARVED WOOD FLUTE

Just before Easter. Half a foot of snow overnight. The boughs of the
spruce trees bent low to the ground, not meditating, no, but practicing
non-meditation, their roots still asleep deep in the still-frozen earth,
morning temperature plunging to thirty below.

Is this the immaculate heart of beauty, this frost-deepened austerity?

Winter wind whipping bare branches does not sing, *Once upon a time*,
or *Forever and forever*, or *Happily Ever After*. Those stories of salvation.

You want to be taken by quiet. What you want in the landscape is
clarity. What it offers—red polls and sparrows bickering over tiny,
frost-blackened apples; geese returning north, dragging their shadows,
babbling as if to assure themselves not only that they exist, but also that
they are not alone.

In your meagre house, in a village on the south Saskatchewan flatlands,
human visitors rare, it is impossible to forget you are immersed in the
turning seasons, your gnomic body a wisp, a twist of cloud. Small house,
two doors, and windows in every wall. Nothing but seeing through and
thresholds. All winter long, cold and snow slipping beneath doors, light
or no light filling windows.

Wherever the mind dwells apart and alone is itself a distant place.

In two months, perhaps you will remember nothing of this day, these
thoughts. Summer will have had its way with everything—there will
be green leaves on the elm, coneflowers blooming yellow, blackbirds
chasing away the crows. You will be able to walk the ditches of the grid
road, sage and willow rooted in the flesh and bones of your ancestors.
And rather than *think*, you will simply *look*—whatever lives in you
concentrated in your eyes.

After so long caged in the traps and pitfalls of mind, the land returns—returns *you* to occurrence arising of itself, out of the void. And just like that, somehow you've found your life again, not having recognized absence until the return.

Perhaps it was never tomorrow or another year you were looking for but simply that single eagle riding the high air, this afternoon, far above the pelvic valley that holds Buffalo Pound Lake. Seven white pelicans afloat, blazing in sun. Pike drowsing in the shallows. Water lapping stones.

These are the things that you know. This is how you make peace with thousand-year-old sorrows. How you keep your empty whole.

SPRING, LOW-PRESSURE SYSTEM

A week of rain at the beginning of May.
Tonight, a single, pale purple-pink plum blossom
against the black, black night.

Do not call it *lonely star*. This might not be a lie
but overhead you have caught in the corner of your eye
a single, distant star, which when you look directly is not there,
visible only to the eye
                    of indirection.
Mind of Indirection,
                    will you get to the point?

The star is not—
It is you who are lonely,
motherless, fatherless orphan-child.
                        Of course,
you are not, could not be without mother, without father, this
just another pose your bored soul, bored full of holes, adopts, once again
in search of ways to amuse itself,
                        immature, un-ripened
fruit that it is.

Yours was no spring
                from nothingness into existence.
No miracle birth beyond any earth-bound womb for you,
no one-upping The Showman's immaculate conception
and return from the tomb.

Christ! What a trick!
                The one they've been talking about ever since—
some claim they still have a copy of the flyers advertising the show
tucked between the pages of a book of myths.
                        A bag of the desert-sun-
roasted peanuts that were sold to the anxious, waiting crowd

at an exorbitant, a blood price.
                          Some claim to hear still
in the still-hearted night
the echoing ring,
the shout:

I've been in the grave! Now I'm out!

Simply put, your father is dead, twenty-one years in the ground now.
Your mother somewhere north, an anchorite of the dense boreal forest,
the last of her husbands down the shaft of a mine soon to die of the
          search for gold.

Your feet are cold as you sit on the back deck with a too-late-for-this-
          time-of-night
cup of coffee and a smoke, five dogs asleep around your chair, aware,
for this moment at least, of the lies on which you subsist, gathering them
like berries in a pail, aware that there is no moment, no isolated particle
in the slow-flow of time, no atom at the heart of things, though
you still name the names.
                    A litany of futility, liturgy of obfuscation.

Aware that time flows like the stones in the rock garden, all movement
nothing more than memory, now, stilled into stasis.
And hard, and unsmiling, and cold.

Yesterday, the first day of spring. Today, large flakes of snow flutter in the absence of wind, drop like ghosts of heavy, wet-winged moths from another world. But there is only this world. No need to grieve.

Look at the chickadees in their black caps, huddled in the spruce tree in the south-west corner of the yard. Listen to the starlings raising a racket in the cottonwood across the street. Take up your walking stick, pull on your boots, and meditate that way—one foot after another. Stop wishing for the sky to clear. Better to clear your mind with walking and breathing—into the open fields, winter stubble and ice cracking beneath your feet, sun a half-remembered dream, possible only in another season.

Being is straightforward: Before you is the field. Behind you is the village where you live. Geese in the distance eating seed. Coyotes hunting geese. Trees and songbirds. Snow on the brim of your hat. Red tail of a fox disappearing into earth. Breath drifting in clouds, up to where no spirits are gathered. Ten thousand thoughts rising from, descending to, the void. Simple.

Return to your small house. Light a fire. Make an offering of tobacco. Burn sweetgrass. The smoke will rise to the rafters of the sky and beyond. Listen to the dogs yelping at two doves hunkered down on the power line. Warm a bowl of soup and eat. Let your home harbor idleness, some peace, a brief respite from the habitual traps of mind.

But then, there's memory. That old ache in the knee. Your father. Your friends. Aunts and uncles and cousins. All the holes you have dug in your heart to bury your dead.

But here's another memory: You stand in the new-moon night—among Ponderosa pine on a mountainside, half a mile above Okanagan Lake, twenty paces from the retreat house—watching the Perseid meteor shower. The falling lights strip you bare of thought, strip you bare of yourself.

March. Try to remember:

For today, there is no need to grieve.

When spring finally arrives, by its own path and in its own time, take to the backyard, try to nurture something like simplicity: Lupine, coneflowers, bergamot, and wild roses. Chokecherries, crab apples, currants, and plums. Rearrange the rocks you have dragged home from the shoreline of Buffalo Pound, the way you rearranged your thoughts, endlessly, in the long hours and days of winter darkness.

At nightfall, when you come tired to your bed, leave your self outside among rocks and roots. There will be sleep. There will be dreams—of a winter yet to come. Fallen seeds. The remnants of clinging fruit to feed the remnants of birds.

You come down the stairs in robe and slippers, old knees croaking, creaking like the wood beneath the worn carpet. Your father sits in the dark at your kitchen table staring out the window, just as you remember him, smoking a Sportsman and drinking coffee. Perhaps it is only his reflection he sees in the midnight glass. His mind and heart, rooms where too much has happened for either of you to bear.

Since you cannot sit with him, you wander out the backdoor to have a cigarette. He will not join you.

Cool damp wind from the west, dew in the grass swallowing starlight. In four hours, the sunrise, both the sun and its light, will already be eight minutes into the past when you see them.

Into the past, as if anything can enter *there*, into *that*.

Apple blossoms in the trees, suffusing the dark with their sweetness, seven blackbirds raising a racket at your presence, while the neighbours sleep. Walk down to the stone-pile where the purple spears of lupine grow. In autumn, you will collect the seeds, dry them in a bowl on the altar where you burn candles, sage, cedar and sweet grass, offerings to your ancestors, and to the Buddhas who hunch there laughing.

You will try to carry one year forward into another. Again, the old ache and yearning for divinity. For absolution, for benediction.

When you return to the house, your father is gone. Again. There is no hole in the air, just the breeze from the doorway that shifts the spider webs you have allowed to multiply in the upper corners of the ceiling, on the blinds and light fixtures. This year, you have discovered cat-faced spiders. Their square-cornered bodies remind you of cardboard folded into boxes, the way a cancerous abdomen protrudes—stiff, rigid— beneath a blue fleece blanket when you hug someone.

There is a trapezoid of moonlight on the square, white kitchen tiles, and you wish geometry could save you. While you puzzle, *nothing*—neither a greater, nor a lesser god— is somewhere else, but nearby, doing whatever it is that *nothing* does.

CREATION STORY

for Isadore Pelletier

This is how it begins,
not with a word, but
with a single breath.

Something our bodies do, not
involuntarily, but without
the intervention of our wills.

Something our bodies do
to save us
from consciousness and death.

Still it is there—death—in that moment
between inhalation and exhalation,
in the time between the separate
beatings of our separate hearts,
in the infinitesimal time
our minds allow our bodies to be.

But, of course, it is our bodies that allow our minds to be,
for a brief time, and always, it is there—
death, like a bird that preys
upon another bird
in mid-flight.

The light this morning is uncanny—thin and grey; the air is stilled.
The trees, even the last three leaves that cling to the ash, are motionless.
If there is a sunrise beyond the cloud cover, it is weak, just enough to
sulfur-tint everything. Is it the scent of brimstone to which the dog
raises its nose? A cloven-footed creature stands just beyond your left
shoulder, sucks the breath from your lungs. But you know the hungry
ghosts and the wihtikows live inside.

It is as if, overnight, this world has ceased to be and become the next.
But nothing ever ends. Take memory. It lives inside, too, not just in
your mind, but in each cell, in the marrow of your bones. Even the
stones, those grandparents, who have emerged in a kind of birth from
beneath the snow in the warm front that arrived overnight, carry
memories. They are not the blind eyes they seem. In their silence, they
are remembering, thinking their way back through crust and mantle to
the iron and nickel core.

They know you, that core and each stone. They exert an intimate
gravitational pull on your body, as do the trees and the small, grey
bodies of the sparrows huddled there. Your body, too, tugs on all the
ten thousand things, as if to wrap itself in a material embrace. Your
heart tugs an inland tide beneath the ice in the lake twenty miles away.
The seeds inside pine cones reach toward each other across the distance
between the northern prairie and your childhood boreal home.

When you were a boy, you could feel the wild rosebuds on the slopes
of the slight valley that holds Cottonwood Creek pulling you south,
toward the muddy, brown water and the muskrats you still watch
swimming there in summer. A red-tailed hawk hovers, holds its
position in the high air. In this season and time, November of your
fiftieth year, the young boy is still alive, wandering the banks of the Fir
River fishing for pike, collecting palm-sized, water-smoothed stones to
carry home in his pockets.

Blake was right, everything is infinite. Even the four-foot cut of birch trunk abandoned beneath the spruce at the west edge of the yard continues its life, though it is no longer adding rings, at least not as far as you can see. But maybe it's a fault in your looking. Look again. Look and listen. Try not to think. Try the meditation of heart-mind. If you listen closely, you will hear the oxidized hinges on the doors of perception squeak, opening and closing, swinging an inch or two, in the just-now rise of wind.

III

Name, Name, Name,
Until You Are Bereft of Words

Late October, a grey sky and drizzle
threatening to turn into snow, all the sharp
edges of the world blurred, the few colours left
faded in the landscape.
One curled, browned leaf on the elm.
Among the shriveled apples, what might be
the dull red breast of a lingering robin.
You wonder what it could be hoping for, this afternoon,
when all waiting must be in vain.

Staring out the window, you listen for the screech of the kettle
like the spring cry of a falcon returning to nest,
steep a cup of green tea to warm your belly,
feet bare on the cold, white kitchen tiles.
All day you have expected nothing to happen,
but when you look again
the leaf has been torn from the branch,
the bird has winged its small, ashen body away.
You throw open the back door,
drag the rag of your mind into the cold,
embrace a new kind of absence,
an absence like that feeling in your hands
after hours of splitting wood,
the ringed, stubborn, tight-fisted strength of birch.

It was still early morning when you put the axe down,
a setting aside of your will, but your hands even now
feel the weight of the steel. In your flesh, in your bones
that dull ache.

At sunrise, marsh marigolds appear
where the deer dipped their muzzles
to drink from the no-moon dark pond.

BEARING STORIES

First coffee, first cigarette.

A slight buzz, full hive—
though, you know,
there is no hive except
the hive of the inner lives of
mind or soul
weaving time, white
matter and antimatter
playing tag.
And then there's this—
a single bee, half
asleep in the half-open
sunflower of early morning,
in the soon-to-come, just-before
frost of early autumn.
Lethargy creeps each day
into the catacombs
of our homes.
Hive and house.

A philosopher once wrote
of humans in a cave, said
we could see only our own
shadows on the rock face.

Perhaps you wander in the chilled
still breath of the rock garden.
Perhaps your lover is lost
in the cold, drafty corridors of sleep,
consciousness cast out, shed like an old self,
the *she* she has become
still becoming.

Perhaps, in the deep cavern of dream
a steady woman's hand paints
animals—
buffalo, deer and horse.
Soon she will rise, hungry, bearing
stories on her lips, in the curve of her hips.
Her eyes gradually grow clear
like water cupped in hands, sediment settling
into the grooves of palms.

Perhaps she recognizes you, speaks
the same language. All the new stories
grow old, all the old stories, once again,
made new.

HOLLOW MAN

You have thought at times that maybe
you could change the world with words,
a thought that must come from
somewhere before and beyond.
Before you bloodied her thighs
with your arrival. Before your father
bloodied her eyes
with his fists. Our veins
drive our thoughts right
through our bones
into the bottoms of our feet.

Where does memory reside?
It builds its home inside,
in our guts, in our knotted,
tangled roots.
Reason has no place here.
Pack it up in a box
with those dusty black-
and-white photographs
on the shelf high in the closet,
above coats no one wears anymore.

We value new life so much
that during birth
there is nothing we won't do
to a woman's body,
to a mother's body
to get the child out of her.

The plants are dreaming
tongues that speak all day,
every hour and every minute.
Wolf willow, sage, wild roses,
gathered from prairie ditches.
Night yelps of coyotes
in the field north of town.

BLACK BEAR

Standing on the bank of the Fir, the surface of the river
aflame in mid-afternoon August sun, casting your line and lure
for that tug that will jerk you out of yourself and into the world.

All at once, as if materializing suddenly from pine shadows, she appears.
In truth, you cannot say how long she has been hunched, watching.

She raises her broad nose, two dark moon nostrils, to taste you in the air,
distinguishes you by sight and scent from trees against which she will rise
to sharpen her claws.

She has learned what she knows
in the deep-sleep dream beneath the surface, in that den
where she has given birth, where she has warmed and nursed
black bodies curled into her own. Month after month,
her body growing thin as the light at winter solstice.
With a huff and a grunt, she rises from her haunches, slowly
ambles away.

You find yourself feeling the land has,
for the first time, looked at you.
And sized you up.

Fox den, dug beneath the fieldstone foundation of the ramshackle barn.
Darkness down among the buffaloberry and caragana roots.
Darkness, hunger, and five pairs of golden eyes.

While the vixen's away, the kits come tumbling out of the den,
chasing one another's tails, red splashes against dun-coloured grass.
Meadowlarks in the stubble field, redpolls on bare branches in the bush.

Dulcimer river of air in the sway of the spruce windbreak.
You return home slowly down the gravel and clay street.
Five dogs wait, read the scent of the outer world.

At dusk the swallows will return, too, cut and slash of wings
as they feed on the invisible. Watching flight,
you find the unbearable becomes slightly more slight.

Aphasia, shadow, and cricket song creep across the lawn.
Dogs sleep at your feet. Your mouth and mind empty of words.
A desert. Pot boiled dry. Sand and silt. Alkali of prehistoric lakebed.

Mineralized tree stumps glint in sunlight, stone
dinosaur eggs in the crumble of cliffs. Distant Gregorian
chant of mourning doves before they sleep.

The black animal a deeper dark
than night, with its full moon light
drifting down like dust
shaken from a tablecloth
in the other world.

You want to sit down at that table
with polished spoons and knives
and eat hard-boiled eggs—white, yellow
moons inside. The smell of freshly
baked bread, a bit of salt.

Nothing but the truth.

Your grandmother's kitchen,
a cup of tea nesting in her weathered hands,
fingers gnarled branches, tangled roots,
shelling peas, planting potatoes, sowing
fine carrot seeds in boreal soil.

I'll tell you what:

a red Ford truck barreling down a grid road
is as close to God as you can get.

Get over it.
You and your God.

Prairie grass, buffalo and beard grass, give way
to hills rising to meet sky and form horizon.
At the edge, leave your mind lying in the juniper
among exposed roots of sage brush.
Your mind, that locked iron box of resentment and ill will.

As you ascend, wind and sand desiccate your spirit,
which becomes hawk, sharp-shinned. Your spirit
brittle as the remains of a mouse—thumbnail-sized skull,
three fine broken ribs, a wind-hollowed femur like the spine
of a flight feather, a few meager bits of brown fur.

Soon you are nothing but body,
empty house of thirsting flesh—muscle and sinew.
The sun lights you like a candle,
a smudge. Burning is your prayer.

You will spend the cold night here,
gather sun-bleached driftwood
to feed a fragile fire as the wind
drops its register from screech to baritone.
Stars are seeds, dormant, waiting for the rain which,
like absolution, will not come again.

Try to sleep, try to dream. It will not be the first time
the desert has thwarted human desire.
The moon rises orange and full, harvest-ready.
In some distant field coyotes gathering around
a low, stretched-hide drum, begin to sing.

If you still feel the need, name the song *Hunger*,
name it *Desire*, name it *Praise*.
Name, name, name, until you are bereft of words.
Nothing to do now but wait.

SON

Do you remember waking up in the middle of that boulevard
in that northern Saskatchewan city?

Leaves stuck to your face, broken twigs of dogwood in your hair.

Smell of shit and piss clinging to you like black mould.

Do you remember falling on your knees and then crawling toward
wherever it was you were trying to go?

Do you remember falling asleep,
the image of your mother's face staring down at you?

Poverty is the natural condition of our souls.

Whatever happened to the blues?

Nothing happened to the blues.

They simply packed their bags and moved north.

They moved into every Indian bar in Canada.

They moved into the Imperial in downtown Winnipeg,

Where your mother sold her dark skin, her almond eyes,
her Mediterranean looks.

When there are no buffalo left,
the people leave. They tie deerhide bags,
take down pine poles that held skin roofs
through those long winter nights.

The stars never asked permission to be here.
Neither did the people.

They gather their children around them,
and the dogs, there are always the dogs.
Then they leave, knowing what they leave behind
won't save them.

SHOOTING STAR

Your mother's mouth
opens in the darkness.
Perhaps a star
falls down her throat.

Once upon a time—
let's invoke that beginning
because beginnings matter.

I drew your body from water.
I stood beside the dusty road.
I sold my body to feed you.
Why do you refuse
to forgive me?

DREAM

There you go again, running down
the stony path that exists
only beneath your seven-year-old feet.
Everything is possible,
but you must open the door.
When you stretch your arm forward,
there's nothing there—
no hand, no knob.

The webs of spiders
this December morning
gather moisture from the air.
Around their emaciated bodies,
a bit of frost like a blanket.

The sun right now
glowing through flakes of snow
blowing off the cottonwoods.
A whole world frozen hard.

How was the diamond cut?
What angle of refraction?
How much weight did it take
to make this light?

BIRTHDAY POEM

Mother's and Father's clasped hands
float like constellations above your newborn head.
Midsummer's apple blossoms, the susurration of deep green leaves
breathing wind, two white dogs asleep in the afternoon shade.
When the breeze subsides, cigarette smoke hangs like stratocumulus
just before rain, a garden of river rock and burnished
fire-bellied volcanic stone hears the call of thunder
and aches to respond. Wolf willow, juniper, and sage ebullient
beneath lightning. In the coneflowers, the saturated euphony of bees.
Humid midnight walk on the grid road, gravel crunching beneath
a pair of cheap hikers that will leave your feet blistered,
the moon distant, the stars close, Sirius, Dog Star,
inviting coyote songs, the far-off whistle of a train.
Nothing but memory now, useless distraction.

Isn't the journey of the mind toward perfection
the clearing away of distractions?

The transit of the earth, the slight tilt of its axis
has given you this, has birthed you into this season.
The silent time, time for your mind to lustrate
in the dark house, with the sinuate, anabiotic trees.
Fogged in, early winter morning, moccasins and tea,
thirteen snow geese barely visible
like the winter sun, overhead.

Let your mind follow them into the fields where they feed
on tiny fists of frozen seeds left over from harvest.

Happy day of birth, happy season of birth,
oh, my nameless one, oh, my unnamable son.

WOMAN HANGING

When you saw the woman
standing in the window
you wondered what she was doing.
It took three or four seconds to realize
she wasn't *standing* but *hanging*.
The problem when you kick
a stool from beneath your feet—
it doesn't always break your neck.
She hung there
—like a photograph
on a wall?
—like an empty bird-feeder
swinging in the February cold?
Your mind reels.

Men came from across the continent
to the town you grew up in
because there was work,
because there was money.
Arms and shoulders
muscled like the thighs of moose—
moose surviving deep snow,
open ice on the lakes.
Wolves followed them
sometimes for weeks.

Women in this town
bought their groceries,
sent their children to school,
washed their floors
always with their eyes lying
in dirty pools at their feet.
They knew where the predators were.
They went to bed with them
every night.

RELIGION

There is a small white church
down at the end of the road.

Pick it up, put it
on your back.

This is what to do
with guilt.

Your mother lay down
in the middle of the highway
waiting for the logging truck
to run her over.

When you were a child,
you stood at the window
wondering why
she wouldn't come back to you.

We don't live in reality,
we live in myths.
We live what we learn,
what we dream.

In the rock garden
a single stone
stares like a blind eye
from beneath the snow.

BEARING

The branch of the green ash
bends imperceptibly beneath the weight of snow.

The moon, full and round, settles its buttocks
just here, just on this branch,
just where you close your fingers
and touch her softly—

just a pinch, just a squeeze.

This is the kind of intimacy
all people should have with celestial bodies.
There are reasons we call them bodies.

Your hand was made for this.

You want to tell your lover
that you envy the dogs.
You have two of them,
black-lipped and hungry—
the way the night sky is
when it reaches down with its tongue
and licks you on the head.
Each morning is new to them.
Breathing is the way
you track one another.

When your time comes
you will go and you will go gently.
There is a threshold.
Take this step.
Someone much wiser than you said
poetry is the practice of dying.

You need to practice more.
You want to flame your life away.
You want to burn.

The mirror you took down today
showed you exactly what you were.
You haven't been the same person since.

You have stepped into the river again.
It is not a mythical river.
It is a real river.
It has a name:
Red Deer.

Your friend tried to swim it once.
It was spring, the water was high.
He didn't make it back.

When your mind bends
beneath the weight of your thoughts
you are just going to have to lift them—
some you will always carry with you,
some you will never be able
to put down.

Heavy, sparrow-breast-grey light,
empty as fog, for days now, maybe weeks,
hard to tell anymore.
How many bottles of whisky has it been?
Whisky, that thin fire, the fire that's flameless.
Heat cannot fool you today,
cannot stop you from acknowledging
the last of the crab apples that never filled.

The wrinkled old-man and -woman faces
of serviceberries, stripped
by scale-legged, beaked angels.
What you really see is birds
who have lost half their weight this winter.
Emaciated deer come to the edge of town to die
when there are no more flower bulbs to disinter.
Nothing for you to do now—
not cry or rage, not
pray or hope.

GEESE

You can stand here,
gaze up at the night sky
watching the Big Dipper rotate
around the lone black-tipped spruce.

What your language cannot reach,
what you cannot see, what you cannot know—
the dark sheen on the back of wings
shedding moonlight as they go.

3:42 a.m. and once again the man cannot sleep.
Coffee heating on the stove,
he's out on the front step for a smoke.

The moon, less than forty-eight hours
past full, is definitely egg-shaped
against indigo sky. Birdsong tumbling
from the branches of maple and elm,
Venus's predawn rising
tugging the sun up on a line.
One more hour before it crowns
the horizon.

He knows the moon's not to blame
for his sleeplessness,
wonders where the trouble lies,
if there is any need to judge.
Insomnia, simply the tailless, one-eyed
stray cat prowling the street again.

The man has been dreaming the same dream
three nights in a row—
he brings the woman
a dress of catalpa leaves,
drapes her in garlands of orchids,
acanthus blossoms
in her hair.
White doves hover just above
each bare shoulder.
Rare feathers bound in gold
shimmer, dance like flames
from each of her ears.
He offers a silver filigreed wooden cup
filled to the brim with wine.

The dream makes no sense to him
since all he's ever been able to bring her
are stories from the north.
His mother, born in a tent, spilled out onto deer hide
covering pine boughs cut for the occasion.
How as a child he gathered gunny sacks
filled with spruce cones
to sell to MacBlo for seedlings
to grow more trees to be cut
to keep the mill open
to keep his father employed.
How he hoped to use the money
to take a girl to a movie.
The deep shadows of the bush
and the darkness of the theatre
his only escapes in that town.

All he has ever been able to bring her
are these stories
and the stories of violence.
His hands shaking with rage

and with drink.
Yesterday he read in a book—
The mind seeks what is dead,
for what is living escapes it.

That's memory for you, he thinks.
Inside now, pouring a first cup of coffee,
the five dogs asleep and the woman, too,
in the room at the top of the stairs.

He knows when she wakes
she will come down to him.
Her eyes will reach for him in a way
that makes him think of a butterfly on a rock.
How it flexes its wings, each tip leaving
a vestige of pollen
like dust on sun-warmed stone.

TWO SHORT MEDITATIONS

for Francie

I

Eyes float
like hunting prairie hawks
in a strong wind.

First this way, then that—
north to south, west to east.

II

Delicate, white Irish hands,
curled mane of flaming hair
whipping in autumn wind.

Where bright white clouds
break and separate,
there is nothing but blue.

NIGHTFALL

Look out
the back window—

arthritic elm,
barren-branched.

Black tree-lung coughs up
smoke and ash.

In last light,
scatter of starlings.

ANOTHER SEASON

Buds on the mountain ash this spring,
a green paler than you have ever seen.

Sunlight, blackbird singing.
What more could you ask, friend?

Pilgrim, what more?

ACKNOWLEDGEMENTS

First, I am grateful to all my ancestors who have given me life, especially my grandparents, and my parents, Marguerite and Elmer. I am grateful as well for those ancestors and relations who are not human beings—the earth, sky, water, wind, animals, birds, plants, stars and planets. They have made these poems. Among these relations I owe special gratitude to my family of canine companions: Alex, Mabel, Graciela, and Reta.

Second, thank you to the press and the people who make it work, especially to Karen Clark, to whom I first spoke about the possibility of finding a home for this project. The biggest thank-you is due to Jan Zwicky for her impeccable reading and precise, elegant suggestions for revision.

Thank you, also, to friend and fellow writer Nathan Mader for his reading of earlier versions of many of these poems. And I remember here all the other friends and supporters who have made life more bearable.

Finally, a thank-you to the editors of magazines and websites where some of these poems first appeared, sometimes in very different versions: *Best Canadian Poetry 2016, Briarpatch, The Malahat Review*, the Parliamentary Poet Laureate website, and *The Puritan*.

Excerpt from "Fourteen Poems Chosen from Moral Proverbs and Folk Songs" from *Times Alone: Selected Poems of Antonio Machado* © Antonio Machado. Translation © 1983 Robert Bly. Published by Wesleyan University Press. Used by permission.

"The Long Walk" takes its title from Jan Zwicky's book, *The Long Walk,* and includes a variation on her phrase "the walk that keeps on walking," from her poem "Into the Gap." Used by permission of the author. © 2016 Jan Zwicky. Reprinted by permission of University of Regina Press.

"When you burn sage, cedar, and braided sweet-grass" (35) uses a variation on a line (a line break is omitted) from Lorna Crozier's poem "The New Day." Excerpted from *Small Mechanics* by Lorna Crozier. © 2011 Lorna Crozier. Reprinted by permission of McClelland & Stewart, a division of Penguin Random House Canada Limited.

RANDY LUNDY is a member of the Barren Lands (Cree) First Nation. Born in northern Manitoba, he has lived most of his life in Saskatchewan. He has published two previous books, *Under the Night Sun* and *Gift of the Hawk*. His work has been widely anthologized.

ᐅᕊᏏᎣ

OSKANA POETRY & POETICS
BOOK SERIES

Publishing new and established authors, Oskana Poetry
& Poetics offers both contemporary poetry at its best
and probing discussions of poetry's cultural role.

Jan Zwicky—*Series Editor*

Advisory Board
Roo Borson
Robert Bringhurst
Laurie D. Graham
Louise Bernice Halfe
Tim Lilburn
Randy Lundy
Daniel David Moses
Duane Niatum
Gary Snyder

For more information about publishing in the series, please see:
www.uofrpress.ca/poetry

PREVIOUS BOOKS IN THE OSKANA POETRY & POETICS BOOK SERIES:

Measures of Astonishment: Poets on Poetry,
presented by the League of Canadian Poets (2016)

The Long Walk, by Jan Zwicky (2016)

Cloud Physics, by Karen Enns (2017)

The House of Charlemagne, by Tim Lilburn (2018)